IBN BATTUTA

The Greatest Traveler of the Muslim World

HENRIETTA TOTH

Rosen
YA™

New York

For my niece Emi, who likes to explore new places

Published in 2018 by The Rosen Publishing Group, Inc.
29 East 21st Street, New York, NY 10010

Copyright © 2018 by The Rosen Publishing Group, Inc.

First Edition

Library of Congress Cataloging-in-Publication Data

Names: Toth, Henrietta, author.
Title: Ibn Battuta : the greatest traveler of the Muslim world / Henrietta Toth.
Description: New York : Rosen Publishing, 2018. | Series: [Spotlight on explorers and colonization] | Includes bibliographical references and index.
Identifiers: LCCN 2016055893 | ISBN 9781508175018 (library bound book) | ISBN 9781508174998 (pbk. book) | ISBN 9781508175001 (6 pack)
Subjects: LCSH: Ibn Batuta, 1304–1377—Juvenile literature. | Travelers—Islamic Empire—Biography—Juvenile literature.
Classification: LCC G93.I24 T68 2018 | DDC 910.92 [B] —dc23
LC record available at https://lccn.loc.gov/2016055893

Manufactured in China

CONTENTS

A MEDIEVAL TRAVELER

Ibn Battuta is the best-known medieval Arab traveler, explorer, and scholar. His full name was Abu Abdullah Muhammad Ibn Battuta. He was the first traveler of the pre-modern age to cover the greatest distances. In 1325, when he was twenty-one years old, Ibn Battuta set out from Morocco. He traveled about 75,000 miles (120,700 kilometers) across more than forty modern-day countries in the Eastern Hemisphere. His trip took nearly thirty years. Ibn Battuta crisscrossed and backtracked across Africa, Asia, and Europe. He journeyed across the Middle East and twice crossed the

Sahara on ambitious, adventurous, and dangerous expeditions.

Ibn Battuta did not explore undiscovered lands. Instead, his travels took him to distant countries settled and governed by Muslims. In the Arabic language the word "quest" (or travels) is the word *rihla*. He traveled within the Islamic world, also called Dar al-Islam. His book is titled *Rihla*, which is a record of different Muslim cultures in the fourteenth century. *Rihla* is considered one of the most famous travel books in history.

A MUSLIM PILGRIM

The main reason Ibn Battuta traveled was to make a pilgrimage. The pilgrimage, or *hajj*, was to the sacred city of Mecca in present-day Saudi Arabia. This hajj fulfilled one of the five sacred pillars, or duties, of Islam. It also fulfilled Ibn Battuta's responsibility as a Muslim to seek knowledge. Ibn Battuta was excited to learn more about Islam and the law. He studied with religious and legal scholars across the Muslim world. During his travels, Ibn Battuta made the pilgrimage to Mecca seven times.

Early in his journey, Ibn Battuta discovered that he liked traveling. He was interested in meeting other pilgrims and

In Mecca, Muslim pilgrims encircle the Ka'bah shrine in the Great Mosque as shown in this nineteenth-century engraving.

travelers and learning about them. He also had a desire to experience Islam in different cultures. In the fourteenth century, Dar al-Islam was vast, extending from southern Spain to Africa, across the Arabian Peninsula, north to Turkey and southern Russia, and south to India, Indonesia, and southern China.

LIFE BEFORE TRAVELS

Ibn Battuta was born on February 24, 1304 in Tangier, Morocco, on the northwest coast of Africa. Ibn Battuta briefly mentions his childhood in the *Rihla*. His family was of Berber descent. They were nomads who traveled the desert on camels and horses. They moved with their tents and made their living through trade. Ibn Battuta's father settled down in Tangier and became a scholar of Islam. Several members of Ibn Battuta's family became Muslim judges, or *qadis*, who presided over religious matters.

Ibn Battuta was educated in the tradition of his Islamic faith. His family expected that he would also become a judge.

The old medina quarter of Ibn Battuta's hometown of Tangier, Morocco, overlooks the Mediterranean Sea and the Spanish coast.

No one knows what Ibn Battuta looked like. A modern-day portrait of Ibn Battuta is displayed at the Ibn Battuta Mall in Dubai, United Arab Emirates. He probably had a beard and wore a traditional long robe and turban. The *Rihla* reveals that Ibn Battuta was charming and opinionated. He also enjoyed having money and living well.

TRAVEL BY LAND AND SEA

During his journey, Ibn Battuta rode camels, donkeys, horses, and mules. He walked and sat on wagons. Sometimes Ibn Battuta joined a caravan of pilgrims. Hundreds of pilgrims traveled together to avoid being robbed and killed by thieves. Ibn Battuta also sailed aboard boats and ships along the coast of Africa, down the Red Sea, and across the Black Sea.

Ibn Battuta trekked over deserts, isolated lands, and mountains. Sometimes travel was easier when following established trade routes like the Silk Road. Local rulers

A camel caravan winds through the sand dunes of the Sahara. Ibn Battuta traveled with large caravans for safety.

protected some expeditions. Travelers risked attacks by pirates, rebels, and nomads and getting caught in rebellions and wars. People drowned in flash floods and aboard sinking ships. Illness, hunger, thirst, heat, and cold made travel miserable. In some years Ibn Battuta journeyed farther distances than in others. He stayed a few weeks to several months or years in a location before moving on.

TRAVELS FROM 1325 TO 1330

In 1325, Ibn Battuta set out alone riding a donkey. In the *Rihla*, Ibn Battuta said he "left Tangier with the intention of going on pilgrimage to Mecca." Ibn Battuta later joined a caravan of pilgrims and travelers for safety. He was appointed a qadi for the group. Ibn Battuta rode along the coast of North Africa toward the learning centers of Alexandria and Cairo in Egypt. Ibn Battuta was impressed by the city of Alexandria and spent several weeks there. He met a Muslim mystic who predicted his future travels. On his way to Cairo in 1326, Ibn Battuta passed

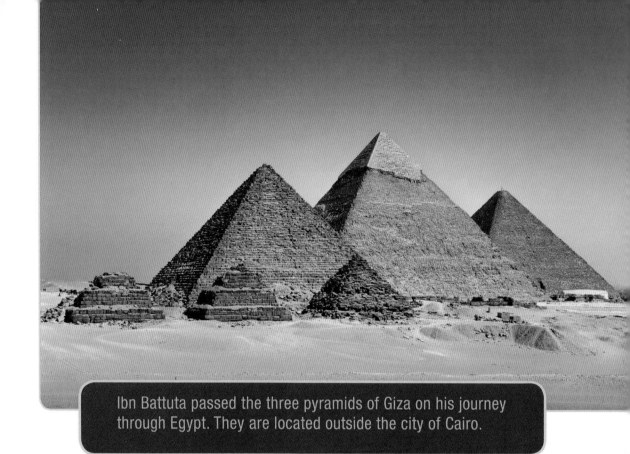

Ibn Battuta passed the three pyramids of Giza on his journey through Egypt. They are located outside the city of Cairo.

the pyramids of Giza. Cairo was the largest capital in the Arab world. Ibn Battuta called it a city of "beauty and splendor."

Next, Ibn Battuta followed the road protected by the sultan of Mamluk. He stopped at the holy sites in Hebron, Jerusalem, and Bethlehem. Ibn Battuta stayed a week in the city of Jerusalem. He visited the Dome of the Rock and the Al-Aqsa Mosque. Ibn Battuta arrived next in Damascus, Syria, a city at the crossroads of

trading routes. He spent a month there studying with scholars and judges.

Ibn Battuta now joined a caravan of several thousand pilgrims. They reached Medina and camped outside the city. Ibn Battuta spent four nights reciting the Quran in the Mosque of the Prophet. The next stop was Mecca, where he stayed three weeks visiting and studying during his first pilgrimage.

Then Ibn Battuta decided to continue traveling. He set out in a caravan for Iran and Iraq. He toured southern Iraq and traveled the Silk Road to Baghdad and Tabriz in Iran. Then he headed back to Mecca for a second pilgrimage. The following year he sailed down the Red Sea in a *dhow*. Next, he explored the eastern coast of Africa.

TRAVELS FROM 1330 TO 1333

Ibn Battuta sailed back to southern Arabia and continued overland on foot. The guide he hired robbed and almost killed him and his traveling companion. In the winter of 1330, Ibn Battuta returned to Mecca for a third pilgrimage. After a year of prayer and study, Ibn Battuta set off for Turkey. He wanted to join a Turkish caravan headed for India so he sailed aboard a galley to the coast of Turkey. He toured several towns, met leaders and scholars, and observed Ramadan.

Toward the end of 1331, Ibn Battuta left for his next destination. He crossed the stormy Black Sea to the busy port of Kaffa

Ibn Battuta is portrayed sitting on the floor praying and reading the Quran. He recited the Quran while worshipping in the Mosque of the Prophet in Medina, Saudi Arabia.

on today's Crimean Peninsula.

Merchants from the steppe grasslands of Eastern Europe and Central Asia traded there. Ibn Battuta heard that the khan of the Golden Horde was beginning a 700-mile (1,126 km) trek to the Volga River. Ibn Battuta and his companions bought animals and three wagons and caught up with the khan's large caravan. This trip took Ibn Battuta to the khan's western part of the Mongol Empire in modern-day Eastern Europe and Russia. It was also the most northern part of his travels.

One morning Ibn Battuta met the khan. He was sitting on a silver throne in the center of a large tent. When the caravan reached southern Russia, Ibn Battuta was chosen to accompany the khan's third wife

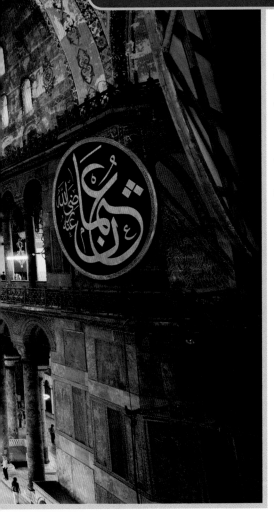

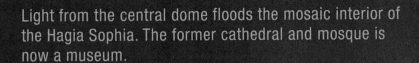
Light from the central dome floods the mosaic interior of the Hagia Sophia. The former cathedral and mosque is now a museum.

to Constantinople. Today, this city is known as Istanbul in Turkey. This was Ibn Battuta's first excursion beyond Dar al-Islam. There, Ibn Battuta met Emperor Andronicus III. He saw the cathedral Hagia Sophia which later became a mosque and is now a museum.

Ibn Battuta next crossed the steppe during harsh winter weather. Turning south, he headed again for India. First, he traveled through the land of the Chagatai khan. Today this includes parts of modern-day Mongolia.

TRAVELS FROM 1333 TO 1346

Ibn Battuta spent two months visiting the Chagatai khan. When Ibn Battuta left, the khan gave him 700 silver dinars. Ibn Battuta hiked across the mountains to Afghanistan. Bandits attacked him and he dodged rockslides. He arrived in India after steering his horse over the snowy Hindu Kush mountain range.

Delhi was the capital of Muslim India. There was also a large Hindu population. The sultan of Delhi hired foreign judges to discourage Hindu rebellions. In 1335, the sultan hired Ibn Battuta as a judge. Ibn Battuta lived a comfortable life in Delhi.

The Hindu Kush in Afghanistan rises in the background of this photo. Ibn Battuta hiked over this mountain range on his way to India.

However, the sultan became an irrational and violent ruler. Ibn Battuta feared for his life and found a way to leave the city. The sultan appointed Ibn Battuta as ambassador to the Mongol court in China.

Ibn Battuta led the group going to China in 1342. Hindu rebels attacked them on the road. Ibn Battuta was robbed and almost killed. He continued the journey by boat. Two of the group's three ships were wrecked

1. Village au bord du Tigre.

2. Vieux Bateaux servant d'Habitations.

de Sainson del.

in a storm in the harbor of Calicut, India. Ibn Battuta missed the surviving ship when it sailed for China. Fearing execution by the sultan of Delhi, Ibn Battuta headed for China on his own by way of the Maldives Islands.

In the Maldives, Ibn Battuta was hired as a chief judge. He married into the royal family. Ibn Battuta made some enemies, and after a year he left the Maldives. His next stop was Sri Lanka and the holy site of Adam's Peak.

By 1344, Ibn Battuta was on his way to Malaysia and Indonesia. He stayed on the island of Sumatra. The sultan supplied a boat for Ibn Battuta's trip to China. Ibn Battuta called China "beautiful," but here he experienced the greatest culture shock. There were small Muslim communities in China, but the Chinese way of worship and life was different.

TRAVELS FROM 1346 TO 1354

In 1346, Ibn Battuta started for home. He sailed south from China to the island of Sumatra. Next, he went to India and headed for Mecca on another pilgrimage. Ibn Battuta sailed the Indian Ocean and then sailed north across the Persian Gulf. He traveled through Iran, Iraq, and the Syrian Desert. When he arrived in Damascus, Syria, he learned that his father had died fifteen years earlier. Ibn Battuta's next stop in Syria was Aleppo and its great citadel.

Ibn Battuta traveled quickly to stay ahead of the Black Death. This plague was killing thousands of people across the Eastern

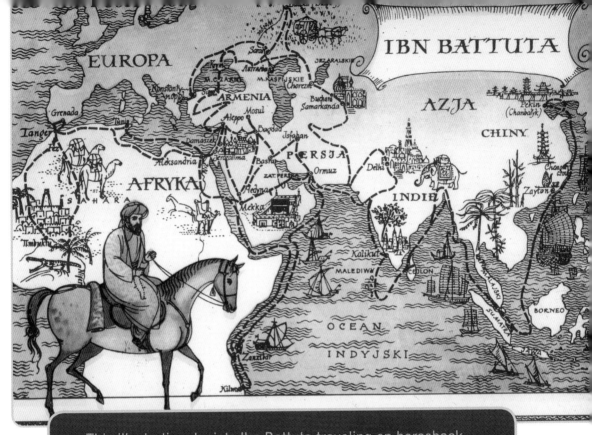

This illustration depicts Ibn Battuta traveling on horseback. The map behind him shows the routes he followed and the countries he visited.

Hemisphere. Ibn Battuta went to Palestine and Cairo, Egypt. He sailed up the Nile River and across the Red Sea. He arrived in Mecca and stayed a few months.

Heading home, Ibn Battuta sailed from Egypt to Tunisia and Algeria. When he reached Morocco in 1349, he learned that his mother had died. He visited family and friends and told them of his adventures.

Soon Ibn Battuta was ready to travel again! He joined a group sailing north to Gibraltar in Muslim Spain. He went to Granada and saw the Alhambra fortress. At the home of a Muslim judge, Ibn Battuta met the writer Ibn Juzayy.

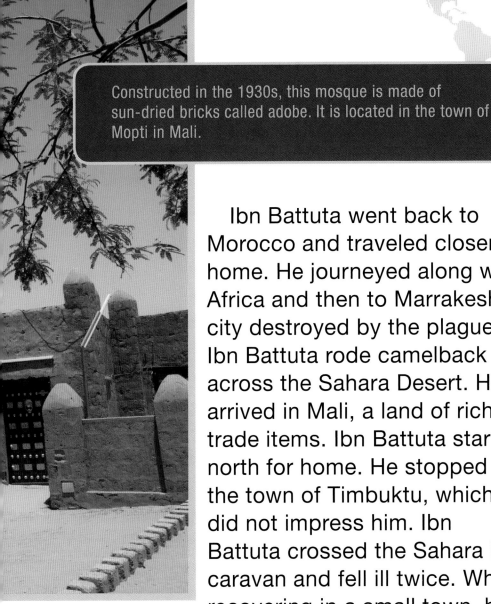

Constructed in the 1930s, this mosque is made of sun-dried bricks called adobe. It is located in the town of Mopti in Mali.

Ibn Battuta went back to Morocco and traveled closer to home. He journeyed along west Africa and then to Marrakesh, a city destroyed by the plague. Ibn Battuta rode camelback across the Sahara Desert. He arrived in Mali, a land of rich trade items. Ibn Battuta started north for home. He stopped in the town of Timbuktu, which did not impress him. Ibn Battuta crossed the Sahara in a caravan and fell ill twice. While recovering in a small town, he received a message. The sultan of Morocco had ordered him to return to Fez to dictate the *Rihla*.

LIFE ON THE ROAD

During Ibn Battuta's time on the road, he met other pilgrims, legal and religious scholars, kings, mystics, princes, sultans, and even whirling dervishes. He lived in dormitories next to mosques, in the homes of scholars and judges, and lodgings built for caravan travelers. Ibn Battuta received certificates of learning from the scholars with whom he studied. Sometimes, he earned his living by working as a judge. Often Ibn Battuta was given clothes, food, and transportation. It was a Muslim tradition to offer charity to pilgrims on a religious quest. Ibn Battuta ate foods common to the places he visited. In Turkey, he ate porridge

Whirling dervishes perform a ritual dance in praise of God by reciting a prayer and whirling into a trancelike state.

and in the Maldives Islands, he ate coconut meat and milk.

Ibn Battuta mentions very little in the *Rihla* about his family life. He was engaged, married, and divorced several times. His wives sometimes traveled with him. Ibn Battuta also had a few children.

ATTITUDES AND OPINIONS

Ibn Battuta's religious beliefs and travels shaped his attitudes and opinions about clothing, family, food, slavery, and women. He experienced culture shock in some lands where Muslim customs were lenient. As a judge, Ibn Battuta enforced Muslim laws in regions recently converted to Islam. He thought that clothing was too revealing in parts of Africa. In Egypt, Ibn Battuta protested the lack of clothing at a public bath.

Ibn Battuta noted that marriages were sometimes temporary, like in the Maldives: "When the ships put in, the crew marry; when they intend to leave they divorce their wives." Ibn Battuta left a wife and son when

Coconut palm trees sway over the beach in the Maldives Islands, where Ibn Battuta stayed for a year.

he continued on his travels. He commented on the behavior of women in different countries. He felt they were too outspoken in Turkey.

Many medieval Muslim lands practiced slavery. Ibn Battuta bought slaves and was given slaves as gifts. He found the foods in some countries offensive to his Muslim diet, like the frogs and pigs eaten in China.

LIFE AFTER TRAVELS

Ibn Battuta fades into history after his long journey. Very little is known about his life after his return to Morocco. By 1356, he had dictated his adventures and experiences for his travel book, *Rihla*. He may have married again and had a family. Ibn Battuta most likely worked as a qadi. His later years may not have been as prosperous. During his travels, Ibn Battuta gained and lost his possessions several times.

The date of Ibn Battuta's death is uncertain. He died in 1368 or 1369, or even possibly in 1377. He might have died from the Black Death. His tomb may be on land

Writer Ibn Juzayy wrote down the adventures and experiences of Ibn Battuta as he dictated them.

his family had owned. Tour guides sometimes point it out to tourists in the medina of Tangier in Morocco. If Ibn Battuta had not dictated the *Rihla*, there might not be a historical record of his remarkable experiences.

THE *RIHLA*

Ibn Battuta did not write down his experiences while traveling. Instead, he dictated the events to writer Ibn Juzayy by order of the sultan of Morocco. Ibn Juzayy wrote in a poetic style. He also filled in gaps where Ibn Battuta's recollections of his adventures were vague after thirty years' time.

The *Rihla*, or *Book of Travels*, did not make a big impact on the Muslim community when it was first published. Scholars rediscovered the book in the nineteenth century. It was translated into other languages, including English, French, and German. Thus, Ibn Battuta

Ibn Battuta is pictured traveling through Egypt in this nineteenth-century lithograph by French illustrator Léon Benett.

and his book became famous in other parts of the world.

Today, the *Rihla* is recognized as a historical record of medieval Muslim lands. It is also an important example of early literature and travel writing. Ibn Battuta said, "I have indeed—praise be to God—attained my desire in this world, which was to travel through the Earth ..."

IBN BATTUTA'S LEGACY

Ibn Battuta's legacy is the extent of his travels and the stories of his experiences. Ibn Battuta was a keen observer of life in different countries. He provided a history and geography of the world of Islam and beyond in the fourteenth century. His account of the east African coast is the only one from that time. His descriptions of cities and important sites provide a contrast between their medieval and modern appearances. Ibn Battuta mentioned the pyramids in Giza, Egypt, and the Ibrahimi Mosque in Hebron, in the West Bank.

Ibn Battuta's journeys were studied in the nineteenth century. The *Rihla* shows that his travels were the beginning of globalization.

The centuries-old Ibrahimi Mosque is in the holy city of Hebron, a Palestinian city in the West Bank. Ibn Battuta described the mosque in the *Rihla*.

Communication and the exchange of ideas between cultures were expanding. Some scholars disputed whether Ibn Battuta visited all the countries he mentioned in the *Rihla*, especially China. There are inconsistencies in Ibn Battuta's descriptions and the years that he traveled. This may be because he dictated his experiences thirty years after they happened.

CELEBRATING IBN BATTUTA

Ibn Battuta's travels are remembered and celebrated today. His name is used for a ferry that sails between Tangier, Morocco, and Spain. The airport in Tangier is called the Ibn Battouta Airport. There is an Ibn Battuta street in Tangier. The Ibn Battuta Mall is in Dubai, United Arab Emirates. A lunar crater was named for him in 1976. The *Ibn Battuta* super dredger ship scoops up sediment from the sea floor. Sometimes Muslim travelers are nicknamed Ibn Battuta.

There is a statue of Ibn Battuta at the Singapore Maritime Museum. Morocco issued a commemorative stamp of Ibn

Ibn Battuta's travels inspired the design of the Ibn Battuta Mall in Dubai, United Arab Emirates. Six shopping courts are named after the countries Ibn Battuta visited.

Battuta in 1963. *Journey to Mecca: In the Footsteps of Ibn Battuta* is a 2009 IMAX movie about Ibn Battuta's first pilgrimage. In 2012, the search engine Google celebrated Ibn Battuta's 708th birthday by posting a Google Doodle on its home page. The interactive doodle showed scenes of the places that Ibn Battuta visited. A 2014 video game called *Unearthed: Trail of Ibn Battuta* follows his travels.

IBN BATTUTA AND MARCO POLO

Ibn Battuta is sometimes compared to Marco Polo, who was another great medieval explorer. Polo started his travels nearly fifty years before Ibn Battuta. Both men journeyed farther than any other explorer of the Middle Ages. Ibn Battuta traveled the farthest, covering three times the distance of Polo.

Ibn Battuta and Polo had purposeful but different journeys. Ibn Battuta set out on a religious pilgrimage through Muslim lands. Polo was a merchant from Venice, Italy, who traveled for trade. They went to some of the same places, like the Middle East and China, and along parts of the Silk Road.

IBN BATTUTA

The Conqueror of the Earth

70 전 1980 조선우표

DPR KOREA

Both men earned respect and worked as envoys for foreign rulers.

Ibn Battuta and Polo influenced other travelers and explorers. They brought back with them information and an awareness of different cultures in other lands. Travelers used parts of Ibn Battuta's *Rihla* as a travel guide. Polo's book, *The Travels of Marco Polo*, influenced explorers such as Christopher Columbus.

GLOSSARY

dhow A boat with a long thin hull often used for transporting trade goods.

dinar A coin used in Islamic currency.

envoy A representative sent from one government to another.

galley An early type of ship that was rowed through the water.

hajj An Islamic religious journey to Mecca required of Muslims.

khan A ruler of central Asian, Turkish, and some Muslim countries.

medina A walled-off section of narrow streets within a city.

mystic A person who claims to be one with God and have spiritual information.

plague A highly contagious infection spread by flea bites.

qadi A judge of Islamic religious law.

Quran The main religious text of the Islamic faith.

Ramadan In Islam, a holy month marked by fasting and prayer.

rihla The Arabic term for travel or quest, usually to learn more about Islam.

steppe A large flat land of grass and few trees.

sultan A Muslim ruler.

whirling dervish A Muslim who gains closeness to God by performing a ritual dance.

Ibn Battuta Mall
Sheikh Zayed Road
Dubai, United Arab Emirates
+971-4-362-1900
Website: http://www.ibnbattutamall.com/en/about-mall
The theme and architecture of this mall's six shopping
    courts highlights Ibn Battuta's adventures and
    experiences on his journeys.

Islamic Supreme Council of Canada
28 Crowfoot Terrace, NW
Calgary, AB T3G 3N8
Canada
(866) 774-7526
Website: http://islamicsupremecouncil.com
This organization fosters an understanding of Islam and
    addresses issues of concern to Canadian Muslims.

Mariners' Museum and Park
100 Museum Drive
Newport News, VA 23606
(757) 596-2222
Website: http://exploration.marinersmuseum.org
    /subject/ibn-battuta
The Ages of Exploration Gallery features the voyages of
    early navigators and travelers, including Ibn Battuta.

Museum of Science and Technology in Islam
4700 King Abdullah Univ. of Science and Technology
Museum and Conference Building 19
Thuwal, Saudi Arabia 23955-6900
+966-12-808-3178
Website: http://museum.kaust.edu.sa/explore-3
    -astronomy.html
The museum's Astronomy and Navigation exhibit
    features the travels of Ibn Battuta.

Muslim Heritage.com
Foundation for Science, Technology and Civilisation
FSTC House, 9 Conyngham Road
Manchester, UK M14 5DX
Website: http://www.muslimheritage.com/search/node
    /Ibn%20Battuta
This online educational community is designed to collect
    information on the golden age of the Muslim world.

Websites

Because of the changing nature of internet links, Rosen
Publishing has developed an online list of websites
related to the subject of this book. This site is updated
regularly. Please use this link to access this list:

http://www.rosenlinks.com/SEC/battuta

Angus, David. *Great Explorers*. Welwyn, UK: Naxos AudioBooks, 2003.

Hardy-Gould, Janet. *The Travels of Ibn Battuta*. New York, NY: Oxford University Press, 2010.

Holub, Joan. *Who Was Marco Polo?* New York, NY: Grosset & Dunlap, 2007.

Jafrey-Razaque, Manaal. *The One: A Children's Storybook About Allah*. Rancho Santa Margarita, CA: Prolance Publishing, 2016.

Jones, Rob Lloyd. *The Story of Islam*. Tulsa, OK: E.D.C. Publishing, 2007.

Khan, Saniyasnain. *Tell Me About Hajj*. Noida, India: Goodword Books, 2015.

Lee, Rev. Samuel, trans. and ed. *The Travels of Ibn Battuta in the Near East, Asia & Africa, 1325–1354*. Mineola, NY: Dover Publications, 2013.

1001 Inventions & Awesome Facts from Muslim Civilization. Washington, DC: National Geographic Kids, 2013.

Rumford, James. *Traveling Man: The Journey of Ibn Battuta, 1325–1354*. Boston, MA: HMH Books for Young Readers, 2004.

Sharafeddine, Fatima. *The Amazing Travels of Ibn Battuta*. Toronto, ON, Canada: Groundwood Books, 2014.

BIBLIOGRAPHY

Aslan, Reza. "World Wanderer." *Time*, July 21, 2011. http://content.time.com/time/specials/packages/article/0,28804,2084273_2084272_2084270,00.html.

Aziz Joudi, Steve. "CNES Celebrates Ibn Battuta." UCLA Center for Near Eastern Studies, February 18, 2005. http://web.international.ucla.edu/institute/article/21016.

Bullis, Douglas. "The Longest Hajj: The Journeys of Ibn Battuta." *Aramco World*, August 2000. http://archive.aramcoworld.com/issue/200004/the.longest.hajj.the.journeys.of.ibn.battuta-editor.s.note.htm.

Dunn, Ross E. *The Adventures of Ibn Battuta: A Muslim Traveler of the Fourteenth Century*, 3rd ed. Oakland, California: University of California Press, 2012.

Mariner's Museum: The Ages of Exploration. "Ibn Battuta." Retrieved November 16, 2016. http://exploration.marinersmuseum.org/subject/ibn-battuta.

Medieval Sourcebook. "Ibn Battuta: Travels in Asia and Africa, 1325–1354." February 2001. http://sourcebooks.fordham.edu/source/1354-ibnbattuta.asp.

ORIAS, University of California, Berkeley. "The Travels of Ibn Battuta." Retrieved November 16, 2016. http://orias.berkeley.edu/resources-teachers/travels-ibn-battuta.

INDEX

About the Author

Henrietta Toth is a writer and editor with nearly twenty years' experience in academic publishing. She enjoys reading and writing about early world history as a career as well as a hobby.

Photo Credits